Alibaba

How Jack Ma Created His Empire
(Jack Ma's Way, best quotes, business
secrets, make money, startup,
investing, tips and tricks, business
plan)

BRAD CLARK

CONTENTS

I think next books will also be interesting for you:

Tony Robbins

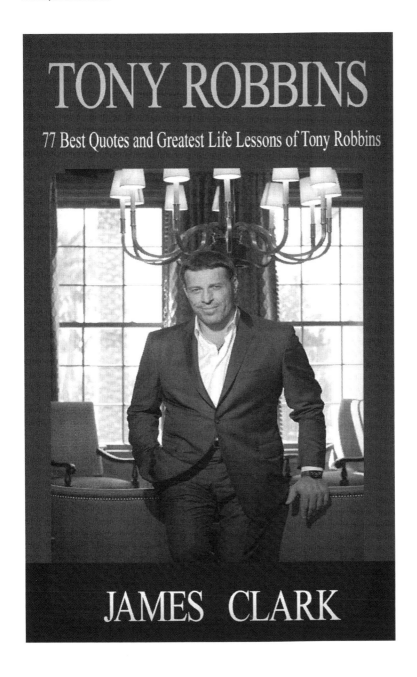

Warren Buffett

Steve Jobs

Business Plan

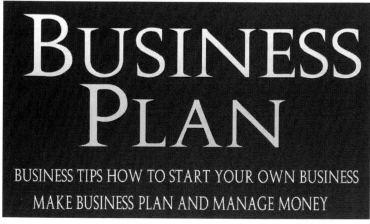

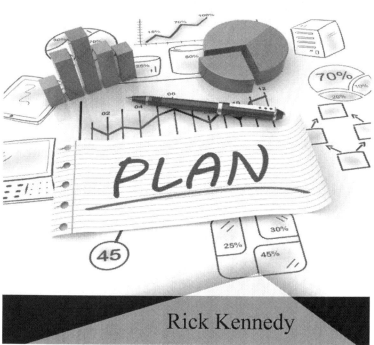

Internet Marketing

Sales

Introduction

Jack Ma, born Ma Yun came into life during China's Cultural Revolution, in 1964's Hangzhou City where his grandparents' political affiliation lead to the family being persecuted for their anti-communist views. This sets an appropriate backdrop for what would motivate and characterize Ma's business life, fighting, failure, rejection, resolve, hard word, vision and agility. Through multiple failures, rejections and even being called 'crazy' Ma has prevailed. His father famously warned him in his youth that his singular business concepts were a dangerous thing in China and in earlier generations would have meant imprisonment.

Yet Ma readily admits his own mistakes, takes ownership of them, does not blame and ceaselessly sees the silver lining. Reflecting on a mistake in 2001 Ma said: 'I told 18 of my fellow comrades whom embarked on the entrepreneurship journey with me that the highest positions they could go was a managerial role. To fill all our Vice President and Senior Executive positions, we would have to hire from external parties.

Years later, those I hired were gone, but those whom I doubted their abilities became Vice Presidents or Directors.'

Being able to put this sort of perspective on less than successful business ideas is something unique to Ma and indicative of his resolve beyond failure.

Chapter 1 – Early Life

Jack Ma, was born Ma Yun in <u>Hangzhou, Zhejiang Province, China</u>. He was raised by parents who were tradition Chinese musician storytellers. When he was still very young Ma became aware of an inner desire to learn English. in 1972 when then-US president Richard Nixon visited Hangzhou, Ma's hometown was suddenly transformed into a tourist mecca.

In hope of becoming conversationally fluent in the language Ma rode each morning, on his bicycle to the hotel near to his home to speak casually with the visiting tourists. In exchange for the 'lessons' Ma would guide the visitors around the city and improve his English at the same time. He struck up a pen pal relationship with one of these tourists and she renamed him 'Jack' as she was unable to pronounce his birth name. Of this time in his life Jack says:

'Those eight years deeply changed me. I started to become more globalized than most Chinese. What I learned from my teachers and books was different from what the foreign visitors told us.'

Some years later Jack Ma would go on to attend Hangzhou Teacher's Institute (as it was then known), even though he failed the entrance exam three times. He did graduate with a Bachelor's degree of English in 1988. During his time at HTI he was elected chairman of the student body. post graduation Ma worked as a lecturer in the school of English and International Trade at the Hangzhou Dianzi University and some time later he also enrolled in the Beijing Cheung Kong Graduate School of Business (CKGSB), graduation in 2006.

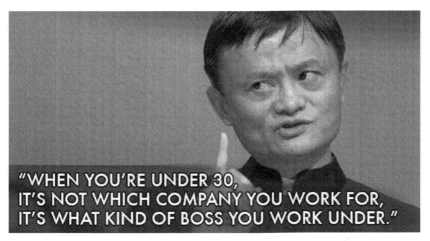

Jack Ma learned the most fundamental parts of life from questioning, observing and experimenting with situations that pushed the status quo. Through this Ma started testing his ability to question, not only the day to day things he was seeing in his country, but also everything he had thought or was told before. This is a practice that Ma still exercises today. About this time in his life Ma states:

'I met a family with two kids from Australia. We became pen pals. In 1985 they invited me to go to Australia for a summer vacation. Those 31 days changed my life. Before I left China, I was educated that China was the richest, happiest country in the world. So when I arrived in Australia, I thought, 'Oh, my God, everything is different from what I was told'. Since then, I started to think differently.'

The questioning and reexamining of issues assists Ma in looking at every situation for different angles to see the opportunities in the problems themselves. An example of this is Alipay, which is a complete reinvention of conducting e-commerce in China. The system was build without the Chinese banking system's approval and at serious risk to Ma's ongoing freedom. Alipay now transacts more business on a global scale than PayPal (using $US).

Of his educational years it could be easily said that Ma received both formal (state schools and universities) education and an even more expansive informal education through the global window his time with foreign tourists gave him and his experience with habitual failure that eventually lead to success. Ma has also stated that the martial art Thai-Chi helps him achieve the balance he gives to both his personal and business lives.

Chapter 2 – Education

Unlike some famous American college drop-outs like, Steve Jobs, Mark Zuckerberg and Bill Gates, Ma was in the process of building what would become Alibaba as he was earning his MBA from Cheung Kong University in the early 2000s. However, Ma is a kindred spirit to these other tech-pioneers in his critical view of traditional teaching methods, most markedly at business schools like the very one that he attended. As a former English teacher, Ma looks back fondly on his time at the head desk and does not rule out another turn at the chalkboard some time later in life.

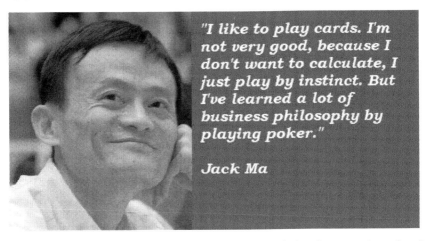

"I like to play cards. I'm not very good, because I don't want to calculate, I just play by instinct. But I've learned a lot of business philosophy by playing poker."

Jack Ma

Ma has spoken openly about his struggles with 'mainstream' academia and, as is typical with many brilliant minds, speaks to the fact that

To excel and succeed, one must have passion for the task and job at hand.

BRAD CLARK

primary and secondary schools, where the most rigor is taken in lesson plans, were his hardest to succeed in. In fact Ma never hides the fact that failure during these years was much more common for him than even the smallest success. What Ma noticed about himself, as he seemed to struggle with 'school minded' tasks yet excel at the English he was learning in his free time, is that he WAS able to apply himself, excel and actually succeed, but only when the task was something he had passion for. Regarding this realization of himself Ma has said:

'If you never tried, how do you know there's no chance?'

"IF YOU DON'T GIVE UP, YOU STILL HAVE A CHANCE. GIVING UP IS THE GREATEST FAILURE."

Jack Ma
ADDICTED2SUCCESS.COM

After his time at University and prior to his going to graduate school Ma applied for and was rejected by no less than 30 different jobs. Although he does not speak fondly of this time, Ma is honest about the way he was received when he showed up for yet another job he wasn't hired for:

'I went for a job with the police; they said, 'you're no good,' I even went to **KFC** when it came to my city. Twenty-four people went for the job. Twenty-three were accepted. I was the only guy that wasn't'

When he was 30 and finished with his undergraduate program, Jack Ma learned about the internet. By early 1995 Ma was traveling to the US and with the help of some friends there he was given his first taste of the world wide web. Being a recently graduated college student Ma's first internet search was for 'beer'. He found a wealth of information about beer from many different places around the world but, obvious only to

12

him it seems, there was an absence of information on beers from China. Intrigued Ma then attempted to search for even the most general information about his home country, to his dismay and wonder he found almost none. Quickly Ma and a friend coded and published a novice website on China. Five hours after the creation hit the internet Chinese people were writing in wanting to know more about Jack and who exactly he was. This was the moment that Ma realized that not only did the internet have tons of information to offer it also held amazing potential for business. Four months into 1995 Ma, his wife and a friend had raised $20000 and began plans for an internet company. The company model was simple, provide a service to create websites for individuals or businesses with a focus on being a simple conglomeration of information that could all be accessed from one place. The called the company, 'China Yellow Pages'. In 3 years' time the simple-idea'd business had made almost 1 million dollars.

"Once in your life , try something. Work Hard at Something. Try to change . Nothing bad can happen."

Jack Ma (Founder Alibaba.com)

Building websites for Chinese companies was something that Ma was not necessarily an expert in, since access to the internet was so limited in China. He enlisted the help of the friends in the US who had first exposed him to the world wide web. This was a very exciting time not only in Ma's life but in Chinese history, of the day they first 'hooked up' Ma says:

'The day we got connected to the Web, I invited friends and TV people over to my house,' (and on a very slow dial-up connection) 'we waited three and a half hours and got half a page.... We drank, watched TV and played cards, waiting. But I was so proud. I proved (to my house guests that) the Internet existed.'

Since that statement Ma has said that he has never really written a single line of code nor ever made a sale to one of his customers. In fact Ma himself never even acquired a computer for the first time until he reached the age of 33.

Chapter 3 – Early Inspiration and Businesses

Ma's frustration with the lack of gainful employment opportunities when he graduated from college lead him to rely on his English skills to teach classes at the university he had so recently attended. At this same time he started providing translation services, it is this job that got Ma to American in 1995 and lead to his 'discovery' of the internet. The business opportunity potential was virtually limitless with the world wide web, and the ability to bring small and medium Chinese businesses to the rest of the world intrigued Ma.

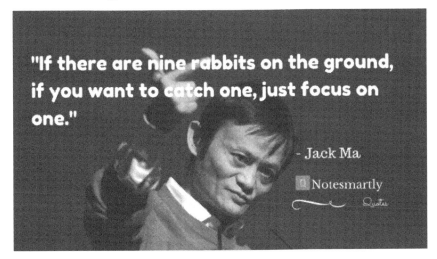

"If there are nine rabbits on the ground, if you want to catch one, just focus on one."

- Jack Ma

Notesmartly

'Chinapage' was launched a short time after Ma's return to China, it featured information about China and listed Chinese products and their manufacturers. Not long, in fact within the same day, Ma began receiving emails from business people all over the world wanting to be his partner. It is here that Jack Ma learned the amazing power of connectivity and gained an understanding for how the internet could greatly impact global trade with it.

You should learn from your competitor, but never copy. Copy and you die. - Jack Ma

After Chinapage had become an established entity, Ma partnered with a governmental entity and lost majority control in the company. Much of Ma's visionary research and many projects were quashed by the stiff bureaucracy of this government partnership. This frustrated Ma and eventually he left the company. Ironically, after his departure from Chinapage, Jack Ma took a job with the government's ministry of foreign trade and economic cooperation for a few years in the late 1990s. Ever the optimistic opportunist, while working for the government, Ma forged many important connections with influential people that later would impact his life and businesses.

Ma was looking for a way to improve the global e-commerce system. In 2003 he founded several auction and payment processing services; Taobao Marketplace, Alipay, Ali Mama and Lynx. After the rapid rise of Taobao, eBay offered to purchase the company. However, Ma rejected their offer.

Jerry Yang, a founding member of Yahoo, is one of these relationships Ma made while working for the government. This helped in the early days of Alibaba when Yang persuaded Yahoo to invest one billion dollars

in 2005 to help the company grow. Using his experience with the government as well as his failed partnership in Chinapage, Ma became educated in the inefficiencies of government and why being in business with them is not a good idea. Reflecting on this time of his life, Ma has said: 'Be in love with the governments, but do not marry them.' To ensure the government's hands-off policy Ma and Alibaba assisted them free of charge when the ticket vending system being used, repeatedly crashed over the annual Chinese spring festival.

Chapter 4 – Alibaba Begins

After leaving the job with the government Ma made a second attempt at an internet based business model. He grouped 18 people together (he and his wife included) at his house and told them about the dream he had called Alibaba. Ma had a vision for small and medium sized, Chinese based businesses, doing business internationally, all through his marketplace. Alibaba brought the dream of using the internet to conduct business globally for Chinese based companies to reality. Alibaba now would also have the benefit of Ma's untempered visionary ideas and innovations.

Early on Ma tried to raise funds as many tech companies do, in Silicon Valley. He was denied and rejected several times with potential backers seeing nothing profitable or sustainable in Jack's Alibaba business model. Ma finally succeeded in securing Goldman Sachs and Softback to invest five million and 20 million dollars, respectively, into the Alibaba 'experiment'. Alibaba was still unprofitable by 2003 which lead to the simultaneous launch of the online auction site Taobao.com as well as several payment processing sites like AliPay.

With Taobao and Alibaba now competing for market share Taoboa's commission free model put a significant financial strain on Alibaba's fledgling finances. In order to remain afloat as Alibaba while still maintaining Taobao's commission free platform Ma and his team started offering peripheral services as a value-add with a small service fee. Some of the items Ma was offering included custom webpages for Alibaba's myriad of online merchants.

In under five years Jack Ma and his team had secured and anchored the Chinese market and eBay was forced to withdraw from China. Ma remembers this time, stating that: 'If eBay are the sharks in the Ocean, We (Alibaba and Taobao) are the crocodiles in the Yangtze River.' Alibaba has parented many subsidiaries and acquisitions through organic growth since it began in Ma's humble apartment.

When the dot-com boom ended just after 2000 Alibaba faced some serious challenges as a direct result of its aggressive, international expansion. Ma has since acknowledged that this was a mistake.

However Ma did successfully reorganize the company's operations which included closing many foreign branches to focus more on strengthening Alibaba's position in its home market of China. Once accomplished, Ma expanded Alibaba's services and reestablished its global expansion strategy.

November 2012 marked the amazing feat of a transacting business volume of over one trillion Yuan. After this happened Ma was nicknamed 'Trillion Hou'.

2014 marked the largest public offering to date at 20 billion dollars, accomplished by listing Alibaba on the New York Stock Exchange. As a 15 year old e-commerce company with origins outside of the United States Alibaba became one of the largest companies when measured by its 200 billion dollar market capitalization.

Ma's vision is to see Alibaba turn into a holding company of massive proportions. The business will be a conglomerate of many technology and logistic companies systematically acquired to fulfill and/or develop certain projects Ma and his teams come up with.

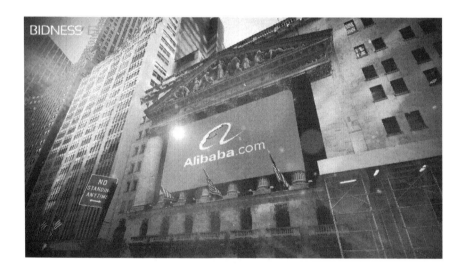

Chapter 5 – Alibaba, an IPO

It was reported that Alibaba had amassed over $25 billion in an Initial Public Offering in September, 2014. Immediately Alibaba became one of the most highly valued tech companies in the world with one of the largest initial public offerings ever.

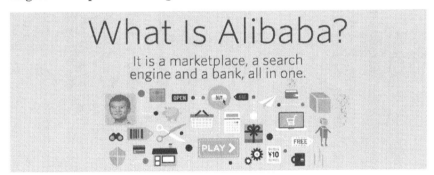

Just after Alibaba's IPO Jack Ma's net worth soared to an amazing 20 billion dollars. The majority of this comes from links to Alibaba and its subsidiaries, Yunfeng Capital and Alipay. Alibaba has holdings in companies that provide venture capital funds, movie studios, Yahoo! China, healthcare technology, phone apps, video streaming and online clothing retailers, just to name a few. Yunfeng is also a venture capital company but it is not partnered with Alibaba for any business. Ma is a flamboyant, energetic and charismatic leader, his influence in business and leadership has been recognized with many honors from very well respected organizations.

Since his flagship's IPO Ma's influence transcends business and moves right into social causes, predominantly in the realm of environmental issues. Ma has been a board member of the Nature Conservancy in China since 2010. Ma has butted heads with the industry of shark fishing, working toward the eradication of shark fin delicacies and dishes. As the chairman of Alibaba Ma has worked to end the shark fin trade and other shark products on Alibaba.

With Jack Ma at the reigns a small percentage of the profits from Alibaba are split off to fund various environmental projects and services. Jack Ma believes in the preservation of life, not just for the birds and bees but for all living creatures on this planet. Once again Ma has begun to bring awareness, this time to China's industrial and manufacturing entrenched economy. Convinced that the world's environmental issues are taking lives, Jack Ma is advocating for China to take more steps towards diversifying its economy and reducing the reliance on manufacturing.

Jack Ma proudly advocates for the fair growth and treatment of women in the business world and beyond. Regarding EOE practices Ma says:

'Within Alibaba Grp., approximately 47% of employees are women, which was brought down from 51% due to the acquisition of other male dominated subsidiaries, and 33% of Alibaba's senior management are women.'

Ma also states that: 'We have many women CEOs, CFOs, directors and so on.'

As Alibaba embraces healthy work and business ethics Ma has fixed his eye on yet a different prize, China's government-dominated banking and financial services industry. Ant Financial services and Yu'E Bao, an Alibaba-associated money market fund are Ma's attempt at using technology to disrupt sectors of the financial services market by offering higher interest on savings amounts and increases liquidity over more traditionally based banks.

"I never thought the money I have belongs to me. It belongs to society."

- Jack Ma

Jack Ma continues to work to use his influence in advancing and encouraging entrepreneurship. He also thinks he may return to teaching someday in his far off future. About teaching, Ma has said:

'For the rest of my life, I want to encourage entrepreneurship, to help more SMEs, and I want to go back to school because I was trained to be a school teacher. I have been doing business for fifteen years, and I think most of the things that I learned from the business school are not correct – I want to go back and share with others.'

May 10, 2013 is the day that Jack Ma stepped down as CEO of Alibaba. He remains the Executive Chairman and actively shapes the group's business strategies and management development. Ma serves on the board of SoftBank Corp as well, the company is in the digital information sector and is traded on the Tokyo Stock Exchange.

Ma is also a Director on the board of Huayi Brothers Media Corp, which is listed on the Shenzhen Stock Exchange. Ma has been involved with the

Nature Conservancy China serving both as a trustee and later as part of the Global Board of Directors since 2010.

Chapter 6 – Views, Accomplishments, Personal Life

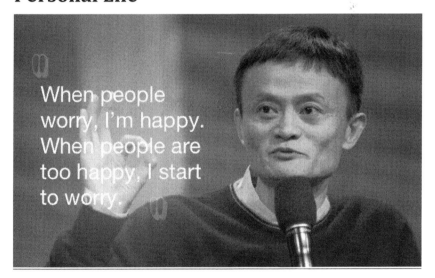

When people worry, I'm happy. When people are too happy, I start to worry.

<u>Views:</u>

- In 2007 Ma told the world that he and his family had sworn off the Chinese delicacy shark fin soup 'now and forever.' Jack Ma has credited this moment with renewing his interest in environmentalism and shaping his future ethos. Alibaba has banned the sale of all shark fin products since 2009 also.
- Ma's drive for sustainability and conservation stretches beyond his domestic projects in China, in New York state Ma recently purchased 28,100 acres of conservation land called Brandon

Park, which sits in the area of the Adirondack mountains.

- In the 2009 Alibaba.com shareholders annual meeting Ma encouraged those who were in attendance to start businesses to deal with the economic downturn instead of waiting for the government's help. The message he used was simple, he reminded all in attendance that the world's great fortunes were made by people who saw opportunity that others did not. The highlighted point was that the current downturn had once again started to show new way to do business.

- In the 2010 Alibaba.com shareholders annual meeting Ma announced that that year Alibaba would begin earmarking .3% of its annual revenue for environmental protection, most projects being completed for water and air quality improvement projects.

- Regarding the future of Alibaba and his continuing vision Ma recently stated: 'our challenge is to help more people to make healthy money, 'sustainable money,' money that is not only good for themselves but also good for the society. That's the transformation we are aiming to make.'

- Ma has said that we wants to build and e-commerce ecosystem where consumers and businesses conduct all aspects of their transactions online. Alibaba has partnered with Yahoo for search and launched its own auction and payment businesses, which brings Ma's vision closer to fruition.

- What is important to life for Jack Ma is that he can accomplish something that may influence China's development and the masses along the way. Ma doesn't change who he is to do this, he just stays himself.

- While it cannot be disputed that Ma is riding a wave of success, his views on starting your own business and advice to new entrepreneurs is grounded in the reality of his early failures: 'What starting your company means: you will lose your stable income, your right to apply for a leave of absence, and your right to get a bonus. However, it also means your income will no longer be limited, you will use your time more effectively, and you will no longer need to beg for favors from people anymore. If you have a different mindset, you will have a different outcome: if you make different choices from your peers, your life will then be different from your peers.'

- Ma's views on opportunity have a similar ring to them: 'If there are over 90% of the crowd saying "Yes" to approving a proposal, I will surely dispose the proposal into the bin. The reason is simple: if there are so many people who thinks that the proposal is good, surely there will be many people who would have been working on it, and the opportunity no longer belongs to us.'

Accomplishments:

You should learn from your competitor, but never copy. Copy and you die. - Jack Ma

- 2004: China Central Television and its viewing public choose Ma to be one of the Top 10 Leaders of the Year
- 2005: At 40 Ma earned praise from the World Economic Forum as one of their Young Global Leaders. That same year Ma was named one of the 25 Most Powerful Business People in Asia by Fortune Magazine.
- 2007: Businessweek selects Ma as a Business Person of the Year
- 2008: Ma is named among the 30 Best CEOs in the World by Barrons
- 2009: Time lists Ma on the Time 100 list of World's Most Influential People. While noting Ma's accomplishments the former Time senior editor noted that: 'the Chinese Internet entrepreneur is soft-spoken and elf-like — and he speaks really good English.' he also remarked that 'Alibaba and Ma's consumer-auction website, Taobao.com, did so well that in 2006, eBay shut down its own site in China. This same year Ma was names on the Top 10 Most Respected Entrepreneurs in China by Forbes China. Again he was recognized by CCTV, this time as their Economic Person of the Year: Business Leaders Decade Award.
- 2010: Jack Ma is selected by Forbes Asia as one of the continent's Heroes of Philanthropy for his contributions to poverty eradication and disaster relief efforts. This same year Ma is appointed to the Global Board of Directors for the Nature

Conservancy
- 2013: Hong King University of Science and Technology awards Ma an honorary doctoral degree. In November, and one day after stepping down at the CEO of Alibaba Ma is named Chairman of the board for The Nature Conservancy's China Program. Ma is the first Chinese citizen to serve on the board.
- 2014: Ma is ranked the 30th most powerful person in the world by Forbes magazine. Businessweek also names Ma one of China's Most Powerful People
- 2015: Jack Ma is given the Entrepreneur of the Year award at The Asian Awards.

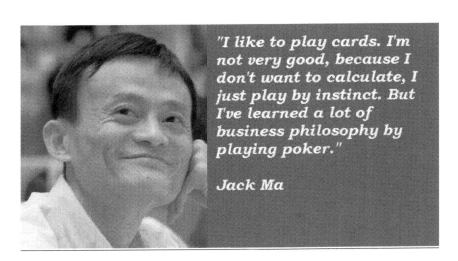

"I like to play cards. I'm not very good, because I don't want to calculate, I just play by instinct. But I've learned a lot of business philosophy by playing poker."

Jack Ma

Personal Life:

Jack Ma met his wife, Zhang Ying while they were both studying at Hangzhou Normal University. They married shortly after they graduated in 1988. Initially both worked as teachers to make a living. The family has welcomed both a son and a daughter into the world.

An avid student of Tai Chi, Ma began studying with the renown Wang Xian in 2009. In 2011 Ma hired a number of tournament winning Tai Chi students to teach the art at Alibaba. Wang, Jet Li and Ma himself teach classed regularly on the Alibaba campus and attendance by employees is mandatory. Ma has said that foremost he would like to be remembered as a Tai Chi master and not solely as the founder of China's biggest internet company.

With his formidable command of the English language, Ma is invited to lecture at universities and business schools all over the United States. Some of his most notable orations have been at: MIT, the Wharton School at U Penn, Harvard and domestically at Peking University.

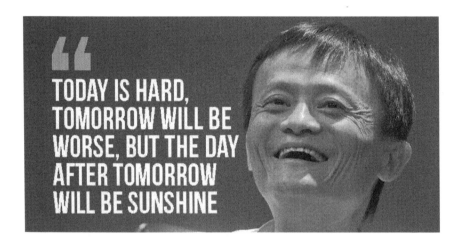

TODAY IS HARD, TOMORROW WILL BE WORSE, BUT THE DAY AFTER TOMORROW WILL BE SUNSHINE

Conclusion

Thus far jack Ma's life is a rags to riches story of the best kind! Growing up in an oppressive, communist China just as it was being opened to the world. Failing not only to get into college but also to find work when it seemed that was the only other, gainful alternative. KFC, the local police, plenty of sales jobs, all these are now notable as places that did not see fit to hire one of the current most powerful and richest men in the modern world.

First with Chinapages and then, soon after Alibaba Ma tasted success and the excitement of innovation within the world of entrepreneurship. When his government partnership proved too stifling Ma founded Alibaba on exactly the opposite principles. But, while pushing the envelope of free thinking in his native China Ma cannot help but remember some poignant words of advice: 'My father said if you were born 30 years ago, you'd probably be in a prison, because the ideas you have are so dangerous.' Ma has an inherent understanding of just how far he can push the Chinese government and sensibilities, he remains careful to avoid statements and/or actions that might jeopardize his business.

Britton Duncan Clark's candid observation of Ma however does show that his time in the Western world as a youth has had lasting effects: 'He is the opposite of stuffy and canned. He's funny, creative and a compelling speaker. I often thought he has another career in stand-up comedy.'

When he resigned as the CEO of Alibaba in 2013, Ma said that it was primarily so that he could investigate more cultural pursuits like education, film making and environmental protection. Ma's concern for the reality of his fellow man is apparent in this quote from an interview in Hong Kong's South China Morning Post: 'One issue facing China is that people's wallets are bulging, but their heads are empty.' Ma is currently said to be working on introducing China's largest charitable foundation in 2017.

Jack Ma shoots for the stars with his feet solidly on the ground. He understands the human condition and the need to feel fulfilled in life. Ma recently summed up his life theory this way:

'But, life is so short. It's all about experience. People seek different views. Some people think you're rich, you're successful, but you're not! Some people say this guy does not have money, he's a terrible guy, but maybe not! Everyone chooses their own life.

I cry [because] we had a lot of problems that nobody ever [imagined]. Because I'm running a company, running 4,000 young people, operating a company for more than 500 million people. [With] 500 million people, if one percent are bad guys, then you have 5 million bad guys. So, it's [a] headache.

But it's too late to regret, forget about regret! Just think, "I've got 10-20 years to go", enjoy the show, enjoy the ride."'

In our super connected, hyper critical, go, go go world it is refreshing to hear that one of the most successful people in the world is human and looks at life much the same way a lot of us do. In a country as large and populated as China running a company like Alibaba could make you ready for any challenge and hungry to start more companies. But while Ma's views on this are optimistic overall, there are four points he highlights as absolute don'ts - even if you are the head of one of the largest companies in the world.

As final words we will leave you with these thoughtful pieces of advice for anyone looking to branch out on their own in the business world:

Jack Ma's Four Don'ts of Entrepreneurship:

1. The scariest things about starting up is the inability to see, to be snobbish, to be unable to understand what is going on, as well as to be unable to keep up with pace.
2. If you do not know where your competitor is, or overconfident and snobbish about your competitor, or are unable to comprehend how your competitor became a real threat, you will surely fall behind him. Don't be the "they" in this idiom: *First they ignore you, then they laugh at you, then they fight you, then you win.*
3. Even if your competitor is still small in size or weak, you should take him seriously and treat him as a giant. Likewise, even if your competitor is massive in size, you shouldn't regard yourself as a weakling.

4. Don't be concerned solely with making money. You cannot be driven by money or you will certainly fail right out of the gate.

Thank you for reading. I hope you enjoy it. I ask you to leave your honest feedback.

Made in the USA
San Bernardino, CA
11 August 2016